Thee Echoes Of My Mind

Thomas Paseka

EXPLORA BOOKS
700 – 838 West Hastings St. Vancouver, BC V6C 0A6
www.explorabooks.com
Phone: (604) 330 6795

Because of the dynamic nature of the Internet, any web addresses or links contained in this book may have changed since publication and may no longer be valid. The views expressed in this work are solely those of the author and do not necessarily reflect the views of the publisher, and the publisher hereby disclaims any responsibility for them.

ISBN: 978-1-998394-90-6 (Paperback)
978-1-998394-91-3 (eBook)

Thee *Echoes* Of My Mind

Thomas Paseka

Contents

Introduction
1

Just Thoughts
7

Chapter 1
The Sand Box
9

Just Thoughts
10

Chapter 2
The Shift Of Innocence
13

Chapter 3
8th Grade-Another Major Shift
16

Chapter 4
Public High School was a Breath of Fresh Air
18

Just My Thoughts
23

Chapter 5
"The Heart Always Speaks Under The Words."
25

Cognitive dissonance
31

Chapter 6
Thee Echos of My Mind
35

Just Thoughts
38

Chapter 7
Aramaic Lord's Prayer Quote
41

Chapter 8
The First Dream Started With Silver Coins
Of All Denominations
48

Chapter 9
Lord's Prayer Aramaic
50

Joy and Peace
54

Chapter 10
The Thunderbird Vision
65

Aramaic Lord's Prayer
61

Chapter 11
The Coyote Dream
63

Chapter 12
The Golden Cobra Dream
66

Introduction

In Thee Echo's Of My Mind the Will of Thee Cosmic Birther… Channels through me. As I am an Instrument of All's Light and Love. In whom I place my Trust and surrender my Will. Thee Cosmic Birther is Thee Alpha and the Omega… Thee Beginning and Thee End… My Lord and My God… My Higher Self… Consciousness… is Thee all-inclusive Essence… ALL. As the wheels of Life turn, I receive Insights to achieve my Purpose… As a cosmic collector, I am to share these messages of All… When Embraced.

This journey began when realizing, I was diverted by the ways of Man and my Ego. I was coming out of the Desert… I had lost my way. This realization came as a Revelation through a Prophecy.

Now I am sharing the Original Prophecy from my five times removed Great Grandmother.

"You (me) receive but you don't put action in place. He (Thomas) is a Tchatche (small gift) that is meant to be more but he receives but does not follow the Path of Enlightenment.

"He chooses to be small by being a caregiver, allowing himself to be used to make himself all important (Ego).

If I (grandmother) had Wheels, I would be a wagon… Meaning… "Don't expect people to do things they aren't equipped to do."

Dogs can be trained to love and follow man.

Man uses those who do not see but only their own impotence, which is melting ice (changes shape and fades).

I am memère, not grand-mère (great-grandmother) …" Old Granny... babicka (grandmother-memere).

"Babi" long before he was wombed. I wombed his father's father: Gifts came through them—gentle strength, caring but fading— wants to be the one who controls, not the one who receives and gives the knowledge & moves on.

Our sensing and knowing ends with him because his self needs to be a Savior; his Ego—you (Joan) know Ego and what it means, but he does not heed what it means.

His need to be the Savior… His humanity is shortened. We will only watch now. No one can come any longer. Old One (Joan), you will come many more times but Thomas will not unless he learns to receive and act and not keep seeking.

He will no longer receive divine guidance—he does not act when given. He is failing as his forerunners.

Tomas could be an Old Soul, but ice is fading because he carries crosses instead of giving his intuitions to others and not becoming involved and letting others grow into trees if it is their destiny.

He chose to carry crosses not to spread the wisdom that was to pass through him. He allows human insecurity to interfere by being a caregiver and stroking another's ego but not seeing it. He was doing so well with his purpose—book… there is blackness—Get Out (personal time to move on).

This is the prophecy.

Then my Higher Self spoke:

"Thomas, I need YOU!

Thomas, I need you!

This calling was the pivotal point.

It took months for me to understand and own the calling.

I asked my Higher Self... Why do you need me? I need you.

You... Thomas, you agreed to serve me... Karma... Be careful what you ask for... as you do not know what you have to experience to fulfill your agreement.

I was totally humbled when I understood and owned my agreement... After I became conscious of what my karma entails. I can see more clearly the prophecy. Now, I am alive and choose to live it... as best as I know how.

Allow... Allow... Allow... ALL to work through me and I through ALL.

Show me... Show me... Show me...

This is my grounding mantra.

O Cosmic Birther of all radiance (Light) and vibration (Love has many facets... known as energy fields such as Chakras). It was an awakening! I needed to put into action to untie the tangled threads of destiny that bind myself as well as others as I release them from the entanglement of past mistakes.

This brought forth the emancipation of the mind as focal point for sharing insights.

To fulfill my purpose through awareness by sharing this truth and that actions speak volumes.

This is the Eye of the Nous... one's heart. It is our Higher Self's place of connection. "The heart always speaks under the words."

Upon understanding this truth... I started to emote. My feelings are triggers of emotional reactions to deeply buried experiences... I have had that are still echoing in my mind from my subconscious.

These memories are keys that have liberated me from human bondage of ignorance by choosing to seek truth.

The energy fields of chaos divert mankind from one's path... causing doubt. All sense of security is challenged. Fear sets in. Facing my fears is the heaviest task I have encountered even in this present moment. The constant bombardment of negative energy from all sources, whether from the collective consciousness or my own personal consciousness, tests everything I believe... in the echoes of my mind. And it is OK... it woke me up!

This world and the universe at this moment are also at the apex of monumental shifts in consciousness... personally and collectively.

The product of the means is the product of the extremes. Meeting in the middle is a path to peace of mind, body, and soul. In fact, it is the road less traveled.

I had been in a good place for a long time. I was living the truth of who I was meant to be... fulfilling my destiny. I published my first book.

Little did I know my biggest challenge was about to happen as I decided to draw from my subconscious. I had received my prophecy... it took me back to my shadows... as my awareness was being focused on the prophecy. Pausing and reflecting, I started with the very first recall I had.

The reflection was when I was about 2 ½ years old. I was helping my dad as he was hoeing and cleaning out the weeds in our garden. Then my grandmother was standing with us. As they chatted, the Hester sisters who lived behind us were approaching the fence that divided the properties.

I am watching this movie as an adult (eating my popcorn). Asking myself... what is the significance of this moment?

As I began to realize I was in a moment of sensing the love that was emanating from my dad, beaming from his sky-blue eyes... as I walked within the row of beans with him. I knew then I was loved and wanted. I could feel it. My heart spoke!

My grandmother also radiated her love on me as I looked into her eyes. This insight, which I received, was an indelible mark on me as I realized my mom had the same energy emanating from her eyes... I am loved and wanted... what a blessing.

As the Hester sisters poured out their acolytes, reinforcing the reflection of this loving moment, I was warm and fuzzy all over... as I am radiating the light and love from my heart at this moment.

Then I paused as I was also sensing another reflection. I did not see my mom. As I began to realize my brother had recently been born. Mom was in our home enjoying the birth of her new son.

Again, I am conscious of the love I was born into—the most important gift of life... to be loved and wanted. My parents loved my two older sisters and their two boys.

This reflection set the pace for how I live my life in the present moment. This is the best and the first movie I recall from the echoes of my mind.

Recalling many movies, I always feel their love and the security of being wanted.

I am smiling as I reflect on this.

My Roman great-grandmother, five times removed, who gave me my prophecy, also gave us the wanderlust. As a family, we traveled. Travel was my dad's gift. He expanded our world, and I ran with it... I was always ready for adventure... be it on the road or in our backyard. I see the magic of life through my dad.

My mom also had that sparkle in her dark brown eyes. Mom expanded us in many different ways—taking us to school, band, church, and all our ups and downs of everyday living… giving me many fond memories right along with my dad. They worked together, giving their best. I loved my time with my mom, even though I was a rascal. Yes, I was a rascal! I was always outspoken. Therefore, I was given the right parents. They gave me good values and a moral compass to live by.

These memories are so precious and important. The security I have to this day… I am loved and have a special sense of being wanted. Even when I am challenged, I reflect and know this is truth. I really had to ground myself in the depiction of my parents. "Never forget where you came from" was and still echoes in me.

Just Thoughts

"Inner beliefs become our outer world."

"Everyone is a reflection.

Reflections are insights.

To the whys of how one reacts

to experiences we have."

"Until a soul feels its worth as a child of the universe,

how can one know

the essence of life is love?"

"The heart always speaks under the word."

Off to the movie, the marquee reads.

The Sand Box

This movie started in the sandbox (Oh! Don't forget your popcorn) that my dad built for me. I was about 3 ½ years old. I had it all to myself. It was a cold day in the spring as I was playing. Suddenly, I looked up, and my dad had my baby brother in his arms as he was approaching me.

My first moment of jealousy that I remember was upon me. I was not a happy camper. I had to share my dad and the sandbox! This reflection was my first conscious experience of sibling rivalry, even though I did not understand the reaction I had at the time. What an impact it left on me... as it was hidden in my subconscious. An old picture of me in the sandbox had reappeared. This reflection initiated the return to the scene... jealousy and resentment. I had to share my dad and my sandbox.

Our special one-on-one times were different after that scene. This brought a flood of reoccurring events throughout my life... in this moment. Number one is sharing and sibling rivalry and how it affected the psyche.

At the end of this movie, I had to process that recall in the present moment as a result of my prophecy.

It was unbelievably hard. I had exposed and accepted my ill ego. In other words... get over yourself.

"Playing safe, like a reprieve,
chance to relax, to catch the breath.
Energy moves forward.
A glimpse allows the move by just being aware."

"Learn not to fear and resist the inevitable discomfort
that is experienced when processing emotions.
It is through experience that one grows."

"We tame our reactions to life
by embracing and reflecting,
until we come to acceptance of what is,
which then eliminates chaos and drama in life."

Just Thoughts

I have apologized to my brother. I am no longer jealous of him. I love you as our father loved us all. A major insight was revealed. I am back on my path with more means to face my shadows... that are from the echoes of my mind.

Intermission

I had a lot of cleaning up to do after that revelation. I am still moving forward... a time to recharge.

Yes... I need to replenish my popcorn!

I am back!

Reflecting is a way of life until one reaches a point of awareness. Having collected and incorporated my insights... I started to open my heart to my awakening from the blockages that keep me tangled in the web of destiny. I was living in chaos.

No longer oblivious to why I was stuck in the ways of man, I have begun to piece together the control methods I hold in my subconscious... one at a time. Liberating the ties that bind me to false beliefs.

Quote page 43

"As long as the mind believes

what it was taught to be good

without questioning,

it can be a deficit to our joy and peace

as it may not be truth."

The Big Bang Theory was over. I have maxed out the limits of man. I was spinning my wheels as I sat in my wagon, realizing I was not going anywhere... always ending in the same place I started... stuck in a limited mindset.

I had to break the chains of human bondage. I was going nowhere, lacking understanding of the force that placed me in a box of limitations... ignorance by shadows.

I was traveling on the yellow brick road... and that is okay. It was a gift of love and light that I am grateful for in all my life journeys, as it has returned me to light and the love at the end of the forest... a meadow.

I was humbled.

I was reaping the fruits of my labor.

Yes, another movie!

A near drowning.

The near drowning is vivid in my mind. Every time I recall it into my consciousness, I rerun the movie as if I am reliving that moment.

As I remember, there was no fear, and I was not traumatized. Actually, the light and the hand of help were gripping my hand and lifting me up out of the water. The shining light was uplifting.

My uncle finished pulling me out of the gravel pit. This is all I remember at the moment. Shortly after that, I see myself in the church I was raised in. I was kneeling with my focus on St. Joseph holding Jesus, remembering my words I spoke: "Lord, I do not know what you want me to do... but I am wanting to do what you ask of me." These reflections have been gifts as I gather them while I write.

"Introspection: the power of self.

How riveting are self-reflections?

Insights ricochet from facet to facet,

until returned to the center of all understanding."

Realizing now, my purpose is to be a messenger. This near death was just one way I was being shown my path. Not realizing, I am a cosmic collector of information that I am to share with others.

At ten years of age, I was still very innocent in my ways. The flashback was monumental as I was living my life. I was very spiritual after the experience at the church.

Seeking knowledge and meaning, I was obsessed with the lives of the saints and what brought them to follow their higher self.

The near drowning was a grounding seed that has now revealed the insight of knowing the purpose. After a year and a half of reflecting on my prophecy, it anchors these revelations to return to my destiny of purpose... to be a messenger and charge the grid of the Earth so the messages can be received.

The Shift Of Innocence

"Do not let us be subdued by that which would divert us from our true purpose, but illuminate the opportunities of the present moments."

Again, at the age of ten, I witnessed an event that was traumatic. My innocence was challenged.

In the fall of my 10th year, a whole new mindset was experienced. Starting the removal of two chestnut trees, as the screech owls had claimed the trees and the annoyance of their screeching.

My dad cut the chestnut trees down and stacked them.

After the trees were cut, I was unaware of what I was going to use them for.

Shortly after stacking the wood, I was outside playing and climbing the stacked wood. All of a sudden, I heard Mom yelling, and she was crying. She had my brother in her arms, running to our house. As I saw the blood running down his face, my older sister was with her. I found out my aunt had hit him in the head with scissors on purpose, and my grandmother was also involved. They were mean to my two siblings.

I was so upset and angry. I started to build a barricade across the path between our homes with the cut wood.

My grandmother saw me building the barricade. Immediately, she approached me. Seeing the fear in her eyes, she knew she had gone too far. As I said, they did not like my two siblings. I loved them... hence the wall... the barricade.

Being so outspoken is an aspect of my character, especially when I witness cruelty and extreme sadness. This flashback was both.

Realizing this, I spoke my mind: "Grandma, you cannot do this to my brother and sister." The hurt I saw in my mom's eyes was devastating to me. At that moment, I divorced my grandmother as my aunt was hiding in her home.

"Grandma, I shall never be close to you again until you two apologize to my mom." And I was not close until she was on her deathbed. I asked my mom if she had, and she did as she was dying. All the hurt they caused for both Mom and Dad... sad and mind-boggling. That changed my destiny with them.

Afterward, I hardly engaged with family... too much chaos.

I share this as I choose not to let this define me or make me bitter. Remembering my mom saying, "You achieve more with honey than vinegar." My dad said, "Do not be like your aunts and uncles." Words of wisdom. I try my best... just some days are hard. Love is forgiveness. Even at a distance... after all, I am human too!

My childhood reflections are vivid, and it is time to move on. We moved away from the family. My dad built my mom's dream home. I loved the new adventures. A whole new topography was at my disposal. The mystery of the woods and fields behind the home was to be explored, and they were. It was our forest, and off we went to play. Mother Nature was an array of animals, ponds of pollywogs, and butterflies. Across the road was the city; we were on the edge of it. St. Johns was growing toward us. It was still more rural, as there was an auction barn where they auctioned horses and sheep. We would go often with Dad for fun, as we loved animals. Riding into town was awesome. We could leave the country and explore the city. What more could you ask for... best of both worlds. Just a flood of memories.

Life was good. We attended a parochial school, except for kindergarten. Our teachers were exceptional, and the system offered many opportunities. Although the school was small, the curriculum was a plus.

My spiritual outlook and my love and compassion were augmented. My faith was solidified. I had a sound foundation.

The promises of love prevailed and still do. The innate sense I have still resonates in me and is a rock to stand on when challenged.

8th Grade-Another Major Shift

After my favorite teacher and also the principal were transferred, Mother Aloysius was the most influential teacher I had during my grade school. She challenged me both academically and spiritually. The reason I remember these teachers is they set the pace for loving school. My first teacher, Miss Evelyn Putman, was so kind and loving. She opened the world of school as exciting and to be enjoyed. Mother Aloysius confirmed her compassion by her teaching skills and the love of her profession; she loved her students. She was always kind and loving—a light that keeps one on the path. The hardest teachers and the frustrated ones taught me to stand up for what was right, even if I defied their authority.

My parents always said if I caused problems for the teacher and was disrespectful, I would be disciplined not only at school but also by my parents.

Well! I defied my 8th-grade teacher and rang the bell for students who rode the public school bus... she was furious. She called my parents. After she said whatever she said, my parents asked me what I did, and I was truthful. There would be no punishment. As I was responsible for ringing the bell to let all the students who rode the bus know they would not miss their ride, as some lived 20 miles out of town. She literally did not care; she was so mad at me. I had to obey her first. I said no. They will miss their bus. So I rang the bell... the rest is history.

I was glad it was the end of the school year, and I graduated from 8th grade. I was to attend a public high school. Responsibility and truth are first and a sound principle to live by.

I hold no resentment, as they have issues too. We all have bad hair days, and I am no saint, and I do not even know what that means.

Public High School was a Breath of Fresh Air

High school was a quantum leap forward. I received so much awareness, realizing the extreme points of view, like enlightenment and shadows. At this stage, I had a grounded sense—an essence of gentle strength and a caring personality that far outweighed my deficits.

As I reflect on the past in real time, my understanding of myself became more objective about life. Before I entered high school, I was not tainted harshly by any of my hurts to keep me from moving on to a new sense of goodness.

The environment of high school enhanced the foundation of sound values I was taught. My consciousness was expanding as I collected and lived life. I was absorbing all the new insights from my subconscious until I understood and owned them, as I have in this moment of sharing.

I honestly am saying my formal education was phenomenal. The school system and teachers were the best... and knowingly exceptional. The universe placed me in an environment of astronomical expansion and knowledge far beyond the average school systems of the times.

I was a good student and was always told I had to go to college by my parents. I never questioned it, as I looked forward to the adventure, knowing college would create new opportunities, as it did.

I am getting ahead of myself.

High school was a necessary step in my walk to take me to new levels of learning, developing my belief and functional knowledge. Starting in my last year, I had peaked again... time to move on!

I was accepted by Michigan State University and earned an academic scholarship that helped pay my way. I was anxious to finish high school. I needed to explore and expand in a bigger world to live and develop my purpose. I had to move on to achieve my dreams. How they were to manifest was my personal reason to walk the good earth.

In this aspect of my life, I had hard lessons. The hardest seem to be the best. The awareness, understanding, and owning the insights that enhanced my way of life for the better are etched in my consciousness.

High school did not challenge me anymore; I reached the point where I was done. The tipping point was the politics, which were obvious, and that is okay. I had bigger dreams and goals.

Even though I didn't fully understand, my higher self was calling me... move on. Knowing I was in search of what this longing was all about and who I am.

As a typical teenager and a blooming young adult, these unknown potentials were planted in my head by my parents.

This mindset prepared me to take the next step, as I was always encouraged and given the opportunity. I am forever grateful to my parents; their vision became mine in my own way.

I did receive my degree from Michigan State University in liberal arts and business. I needed the business degree, as it was practical for any field I would embrace. The liberal arts degree

was my key to my enlightenment and the means to a more rounded life, as I would always seek my higher purpose.

Again... it was not my ultimate way to fulfill my journey. I just had more knowledge to assist me as I journeyed. When I finally tried a field I would never have thought of pursuing, I would have said, "I don't think so!" But I did! I became a hair designer.

At first, I did not think I was artistic enough or felt it was my calling, nor did I realize how it would change my life. In fact, I said to my partner, "I shall try the hair world. If I don't like it, I will walk away and pursue another field."

At first, I was like a fish out of water, being all thumbs. I questioned myself. Then one day, it all came together... not only did I like it, I started to enjoy the creativity. I really love psychology and writing.

My business background just made sense. Business was practical, as I needed the knowledge to run a business no matter what I would choose as my profession.

I grew confident in my choice. Why I doubted myself, I didn't understand until I recalled my first-grade teacher belittling me one day in class. I was combing a classmate's hair, and she emphatically said, "Boys do not comb girls' hair." Realizing that memory influenced how I approach hair... especially long hair. The reflection did not stop me. I had a gift for what I came to enjoy... cutting and coloring the most. A career that took me around the world, literally and figuratively. I would say... and I never left my chair.

I started to apply my education as I became comfortable and had trainers that talked geometry. I ran with it. It brought physics and psychology into the equation. I was in awe of the association to hair.

And when I owned my own business, I could explain cutting in mathematical terms as I taught my staff. That is what Paul

Mitchell used when I went to London to train at his school. I was on the same page as he was. My confidence went off the wall. I was applying the sciences I studied. Color was my specialty, and I had studied basic chemistry. My dad always said they cannot take your education away from you. What a profound insight he gave me. When I started to work in the hair world, people

assumed it was a simple job. No one with a university education would choose it as a profession. That was all changing. Using my education and sharing my background with my clients shocked them. It helped change their thinking about the profession I was working in. Now, a colorist who likes chemistry and color has a decisive advantage to use their talents and apply them to hair. We have come a long way. It is a privilege to witness and be part of it. Loving what one does is a gift. Again, my dad said you are never too good to do any type of work... just make sure you have a choice... get

an education. To love your work makes your career exciting and enjoyable compared to a job you dislike, as it is a long, arduous career and wearing on your psyche.

Hair also gave me a common sense approach to applying psychology. I became a street psychologist. I told my clients I had this connection with that I polished halos and worked beneath the roots. I would not change my experiences for anything.

I am slowly closing the door on my hair career now. I still have another passion greater than hair. I want to write and produce a book, and I have: "Just Thoughts." Being a hair designer was a major contribution to my reason and means of achieving this goal. What my clients shared with me set my focus. I come to a conclusion... truth has no shadow.

Everyone needs to be heard.

I am alive.

Live in kindness.

Balance from within.

This led me to my ultimate purpose: I am a messenger for my higher self... my creator. I am to share the intuitions I receive with the world... that was the message from my prophecy. I have been so blessed, no matter what I experienced... good, bad, or indifferent.

In fact, like all of us, life tests us in everything we know, experience, and believe for the good of all when embraced in AHA moments and all our bad hair days, whether a woman or a man.

Just my Thoughts

In the moment of seeming defeat,
ready to quit your pursuit.
Usually, it is just before a
miracle happens.

Do not cave in.
Rely on the universe once more.
"When facing life,
ask what it is teaching me,
not what it is taking from me."

"I am not broken.
I am just fine-tuning myself,
my glitches."

"Do not be upset;
things do get better.
It may be stormy now,
but it cannot rain forever."

"What we fight are keys
to our awakening."

A new day... I am able to begin as I am awakening... and grateful as well, thankful for the opportunity to grow, expand, and be endowed with the wisdom to understand and share what is to be shown to kindred souls. So we can be a light for the greater good of all, so that each of us has our needs met to grow and flourish. Even if we never speak a word... it is enough, as it is through the eye of the nous (our heart) that we speak and bond knowingly.

"The Heart always speaks under the words."

Filling us with our higher self's creativity that empowers us to bear the fruit of our gifts, which are insights we are given to fulfill our mission while we walk the earth.

"Mankind is the ground floor

for the coalescence of the conscious

unconscious into a unified field."

"Look through your heart, not your eyes.

One is to be in awe of what can be seen.

Allow... allow... allow."

"Surrender the mind to infinite intelligence.

Create a pathway to the limits of the intellect,

through which one can remove the clutter of the mind."

"Life is a collection of reflections

until I arrive at a turning point...

grasping the meaning of my personal reflections of who I am."

****

After living in Hawaii for nearly 25 years... life had changed. My partner of 36 years had passed. We came together to live our dream on a Robinson Crusoe island.

I left Hawaii alone... my journey was completed. I always knew I had more to do. Our daughter knew I would return alone and had shared this with me.

Several of my friends left at the same time; we all gathered together in San Diego before we embarked on new adventures. We were all excited, even though we did not know what was to be or when we would see each other again.

Finally, my car arrived from Honolulu, and it was time to say Aloha and begin our new journey.

All was good.

I had decided to drive across the country. I had no idea how long I would be on the road.

My journey was one of visiting places I had traveled to as a child, including new areas and old friends. I had no time limit. In fact, it was a five-week adventure before I arrived in Michigan, my home state—a journey I shall never forget.

I met several people from all walks of life whom I would never have met if I had not driven across the country, seeing the world through different eyes as kindred souls. I drove many country roads, experiencing places I would not have seen on expressways.

My final visit was with a friend from Michigan whom I was seeing for the first time in 35 years. She lived in Dallas, and I was going to stay for a few days. That did not work out.

Hurricane Katrina was directly headed toward Dallas. My instincts said to leave now, and I was glad I listened. The chaos was already apparent in the city. People were flowing into Dallas for relief and shelter.

After leaving, I decided I was ready to complete my journey. My destination was upstate Michigan, taking Highway 2 across the upper peninsula and bypassing Chicago. I had family in Lakes of the North, and I decided to live there.

I settled in Bellaire, a village of 1,042 people near Torch Lake. I chose a place where I knew no one, needing time and space to collect my thoughts and adjust to the drastic change in my life. After all, I had lived in the 11th largest city in the nation—Honolulu—for the last five years. My main location of business and home for years was Kailua-Lanikai.

Bellaire was like a retreat. I explored the area and enjoyed the solitude, as I was still miles from the rest of my family. My mom and my daughter lived in Lansing. I didn't know if I would choose to live in Lansing again; the area had changed a lot, and all my best friends had moved out of state. I had no draw to the vibes anymore, and that is okay!

More importantly, I had written my first book—that was my passion. I lived my dream: Just Thoughts. Finally, I achieved my goal after 25 years of writing.

Abruptly, my life changed. I met a new friend. Before I left Hawaii, I was told that I would. After a while, I decided if it happens, fine. If not, that was okay. I was used to living by myself, as I enjoyed it. I was too busy to be lonely. I traveled a lot and spent time with my family. They loved visiting me, as the Bellaire area was fun and beautiful, being a resort town year-round.

I did have a few really good friends in the area, and I would on occasion visit them, especially Joan. She was one of my clients. We shared a lot about our interests in our spiritual lives.

On one occasion, I was staying with her; I would do her hair and stay a few days. One time, after we caught up on the new events in our lives, she said, "I have something I need to share with you." It was a prophecy for me.

It was from my five-times-removed great-grandmother that really caught my attention. Even better than that, she wrote it all in her sleep. She discerned it for me, as my grandmother did not speak English, making it hard to piece together since some of the words were in the Czech language. I wrote the prophecy at the beginning of the book if you wish to refresh your memory of it.

After we discussed her message and finished, it was time to go home. I had a three-hour drive ahead. Needlessly to say, I had a lot to decipher as I was returning home. All was not understood during my drive.

I spent over a year really owning what was said.

The statement that was stuck in my thoughts was, "Thomas! I need you." "Thomas, I need you." Until I realized what the meaning was for me, I was lost for words. Finally, I said, "God! Why do you need me? I need you!" At last, I grasped the message. God's answer was, "It is your karma. You are to receive my intuitions and share them with those who are interested. Thomas, you made an agreement to be my messenger and help them choose their own path. That is your karma, and then you would have done my will. It is their own choice how one responds to the intuitions." I had my eyes wide open from then on. I am not God!

My personal message was that I needed to go within and ponder my shadow, as I had lost my way.

I wanted to explain and direct their way. I was not aware of what I was doing. It was a 360-degree turnabout. My guidance ends after the sharing. I was cut off from the angels and the Holy Spirit.

"The Heart always speaks under the words."

I was in the desert—a barren state of my mind. Until I understood and owned the significance of my purpose, I did not receive insights.

Now I was able to make a decision—one, if not the hardest, I have encountered in this moment.

I thought I was on the right path until now. From this point on, I back off and wrap those in the light and love of their Creator and place all in God's hands. I cannot say these words enough when I regress until I return to my new mindset. My means to achieve this was to go within. Our Creator had carved out a space in each of us to retreat—our heart.

"One does not usually allow enough time to know the higher self."

"The heart always speaks under the words."

Shortly after my revelation, I received the translation of the Aramaic "The Lord's Prayer" in English. The translation had a profound effect. It was transformational. My ego was exposed and under scrutiny. I did not understand or consider the role it was playing in this revelation I received. I saw too much; I was obsessed with sharing. I assumed that others would understand as I did, when in reality, others thought I was weird. They just did not see the world as I do.

"Ego is the defense mechanism employed when lacking insights to understand truth."

When my partner, shortly before passing, revealed to me what others said about me, it was devastating. I retreated inward. I was so hurt. I built a steel wall around my heart as a shield to protect my feelings. This reaction was a learned way of dealing with hurt time after time, thus buried in my subconscious and building a bigger shield around my heart (I call it fat and feeling sorry for myself!). Finally, through reflecting and asking for guidance, I started to receive insights again. I faced my shadows. Fear was my blockage. Afraid to face the unknown became my reality. I said to myself, "Your reaction to hurts or any confirmation was harsh." I had no understanding of why I was so defensive in those moments— overbearing and controlling at times as my way of reacting to hurt or anger. What a vicious cycle of responding.

"We tame our reactions to life by embracing and reflecting until we come to acceptance of what is, which then eliminates the chaos and drama in life."

The mind is the mediator between facts and lies, holding one from their true self.

Owning the lessons and understanding them is a must to move forward. Hence, removing the hurt or anger by facing my ill ego and dismantling it to the light of truth… as love conquers all because true love is to forgive others and one's self.

"Until a soul feels its worth as a child of the universe, how can one know the essence of life is peace?"

Cognitive dissonance:

A feeling of discomfort

when holding two or more conflicting

ideas, beliefs, and values.

Holding on to the aspects

are reactions used to escape discomfort

from the chaos of inner conflict.

"One cannot extract from another

anything that one has not removed from themselves."

****

HO' ANO is Hawaiian, meaning the making of the seed. The first seeds I planted were in the last year at the university. Aware and humble, in this moment the seeds are trust and surrendering my will. The journey was long and never-ending, as there is so much to experience, as I know now, as the truth is revealed.

As I am humbled, the sense of the meaning of an awe-inspired reverence is eye-opening. The reference to fear was perplexing, and I struggled with the use of the word. Until I realized I respected the words awe-inspired reverence as a humbling and profound respect from the revelations of my higher self. I turned the page... As I am facing the blockages that keep one in the state of fear.

"Do not let us be seduced by that which would divert us from the true purpose but illuminate us with the opportunity of the present moment." (Thee Aramaic Lord's Prayer)

If the limits of the spaceship (my body) I inhabit are diverted from its purpose, I say, "Show me... Show me... Show me," realizing I need to refresh my memory.

I am regressing to my old thought patterns. The awareness of the mindset I am trying to change is creeping back. No longer fearful, I start to return to the new insights I have been shown.

To know the truth is so liberating and humbling. It reinforces my interpretation of awe-inspired reverence.

This new awareness has humbled me. The truth has grounded me as it unfolds, and I understand and own the intuitions I received, and my actions speak louder than my words.

A common ground has been found in one, even when it hurts and is hard to accept. I surrender willingly, as I am determined. The dark shadow of my mind rules until I face my deficits. Awe-inspired reverence is humbling and the vanguard, the first line of defense in the battle of my mind when lost in the echoes of my mind.

My prophecy was the beginning of the end, the Big Bang theory for me. The force of my purpose is my gig. The must to go within is paramount to succeed in my life, and I sense that more are realizing man cannot answer all that is to be known until one seeks the ways and means to come to inner peace. It is the chaos that reigns as a result of untold truths. The intuitions that are now being shared are driving the need in real time to expose the deception of man.

As more people become conscious that we have more in common than differences, this awakening is growing. Know we are not alone or bizarre, as we have been made to feel or believe ourselves to be. We do not walk alone. Yes, I am the only one that walks in my shoes, as you do also. The soles of our shoes can bring like souls together for the good of all. As we shine and share the common ground of essence in us without saying a word. It is the radiance of the heart, the energy field of love that vibrates and electrifies most as we radiate this common truth to unite us and not to divide us. Compassion with a purpose is a byproduct of forgiveness.

"Untie the tangled threads of destiny that bind us, as we release others from the entanglement of past mistakes."

So speaks the prophecy given to me, the intuitions that stopped me in my tracks, igniting in me to seek the meaning of the intuitions and live the words spoken. Allowing myself to surrender my will to the will of my Creator, calling out frequently, "Show me... Show me... Show me," as my Creator works through me.

"Soften the ground of our being and carve out a space within us where your presence can abide." (Aramaic Lord's Prayer)

The spaceship I call my body has that within me—our heart—the space where a unified force resides and radiates the light and love to others and into the universe from each of us when engaged.

****

As the winds of change are spinning the windmill that brings forth the living waters of the earth and absorbs the fire of light, together in unison, creating the nourishing foods to feed the mind, body, and soul, bringing forth the insights of consciousness that are drawn from the wisdom of the spirit of Mother Earth that bear the fruits of the good earth that are necessary on the road less traveled to fulfill one's purpose.

The heart is the means of integrating the universe with the earth by breathing in the breath of life and exhaling the toxins that stop one from knowing that consciousness is the liberator of the soul as one understands and owns the revelation of awareness.

Knowing I am not in control of my timeline, I was foretold of the consequences of being sidetracked from my purpose—as a messenger only to share my insights. Every person has their own destiny to fulfill and the right to do so, or like "melting ice, I shall fade and leave this earth (die)."

I chose to move on after sharing my intuitions that channeled through me so I can charge the grid of the earth as I pass through on my journey.

"Thomas! I need you!" "Thomas! I need you!" This calling was haunting! I stopped and returned to my purpose. I surrendered my will and placed my trust in my higher self.

As I am getting over myself and placed my ill ego in check, I am not a savior. I am like anyone.

"The heart of love hugs me,

as the winds of change lift me…

howling…

sings the song of love.

Hugs me again…

releases me…

whispering…

Carry on!

Love conquers all."

Thee Echoes of My Mind

Discerning the prophecy is a work in progress. Being insightful, it is like a tsunami; it comes in waves, building in height and force, destroying everything in its way. This facet was based on my awareness that I was to be destroyed, as in death, and lost to my purpose.

Awareness is a constant factor necessary to understand the potential consequences of one's actions and reactions. To stay in touch with one's self is not a fear-based concept. In fact, it is an awe-inspired reverence of accepting my challenges and facing them by being in the moment and owning the awareness to move forward… as everyone walks to the beat of their own drum.

As the tsunami retreated, all my earthly limits were mind-blowing as I was awakening to my shadows. How could trying to help people be a blockage? I asked myself many times. The revelation was: I did not ask them if I could share with them and enter their space. I assumed it was okay!

My ego would get in my way. I had to understand what my ego was doing, and I could not progress into the light of knowing until I realized I had a broken heart. Not receiving the truth gracefully, I was hurt. The people I thought I was doing good for liked all my help but did not understand my thoughts. Later I realized it was making me somewhat bitter. I became a victim, and I am different. Ouch!

After my partner passed, I moved on. The consciousness of old hurts returned to the archives of the subconscious or the clouds. Adjusting to being on my own and where I was going was my concern. My physical world was in order, and my spiritual outlook carried me forward. In this moment, I achieved my purpose. My first book was published and shared with the world, and I was back on track.

My partner always said I was from another planet… like Neptune. It softened the response I had; I just laughed, oblivious to the real connotations. Ego blinded me to self-importance… OMG—I got it! Lost and still hiding behind my ego, my defense mechanism for what I do not understand or own has now been brought into my awareness. Free at last! From Thee Echoes of My Mind.

****

Finally, I found a new friend. We started to buy condos and renovate them into rentals. Eventually, I knew I would leave Hawaii. I seriously started to look for a new place to transition. I considered San Felipe, Mexico, on the Sea of Cortez. I actually bought a lot and had a home designed. It was beautiful, and I was excited. Later on, everything I planned was saying no. Deciding I was not going to live there, I sold the property.

When the time came to move from Hawaii, I decided to return to Michigan near family. I finally settled in Bellaire, Michigan, near Torch Lake. It was a small village of 1,042 people, extremely different from Honolulu. I really liked the village. It was my retreat where I seriously started to write my book.

After approximately 10 years, I moved to Grand Ledge, Michigan, near Lansing to be closer to my daughter. I was ready; I had settled in and started a new phase of my life. In 2017, I finally published my first book and was doing well. I also met a new friend to hang out with. All my close friends lived on the West Coast by this time.

The significance of this meeting was life-altering and needed to develop my awareness so I could grow in my search for meaning in life at this stage. It was, and still is, a monumental awakening to the shadows of my life. From this friendship would eventually come my prophecy. Everything I am sharing evolved out of this meeting and still does.

What path am I going to choose? Am I going to remain a small sparrow (a small gift) and be a caregiver, allowing my ego to keep me in bondage and lose myself and my purpose? No way! The alternative is to be an eagle (my true gift) and soar between the heavens and the earth as the messenger I am to be.

As I said, it took over 2 years for me to really grasp the prophecy and make an informed decision. Now I am living my purpose as a messenger fulfilling karma as I agreed with my Creator.

Quote page 36 jts

Just thoughts

"Until we balance our soul,

events do not change.

Demonstrations are changing situations,

becoming more intense,

demanding and felt,

until the soul integrates truth."

Quote page 37 jts

"Cognitive dissonance:

a feeling of discomfort

when two or more conflicting

ideas, beliefs, and values.

Holding on to the aspect

is a reaction used to escape

discomfort,

from the chaos of inner conflict."

Quote page 14 jts

"Vibrational consciousness is different.

Like vibration, connections create

anything is possible.

Different vibrations in one's path

are intuitively sensed.

Interpretation or course of action

at the moment need not always

be understood.

Just file in your memories until needed."

Quote page 20 jts

"The Heart always speaks under the words."

****

Finally, I am aware that the dichotomy of light and shadows is an inherited mindset. No longer does the connotation leave me sitting on the fence of doubt. To see one's shadow is when light is behind you. Otherwise, one is not aware of a shadow. Therefore, I am walking in light. Upon seeing a shadow, this can be a moment of awareness of a lesson to be resolved. Such is the one I received in my prophecy… I have a gentle strength and caring essence, a gift from my forefathers. Then I am facing the shadow of the ego that has darkened my path of purpose, saying I am fading like melting ice (dying). The shadow of the ego hovered over me for months as I could not grasp its meaning as a savior complex until this moment.

I share my gift as it is a love of people driving me. Finally realizing it was the obsession of helping that was relentless… as I did not know when to stop. I discovered I am to share my intuitions when the opportunity is presented. Everyone has their own destiny to live, and they are the only ones who can fulfill it. I cannot walk in their shoes.

To choose words of guidance was very important in this moment, as the revelation was paramount to my understanding. Asking every day my Higher Self... show me... show me... show me how to be a better person. Let me be a beacon of light. I place my trust in my Creator, and I surrender my will also. Until I realized that I am not alone. I was living in chaos and unhappy. Everything I believed was being challenged. And that is OK.

Living in the light of compassion and forgiveness is heartfelt as I wrap others in love and light, placing them in the hands of our Creator. Destiny is our uniqueness of purpose.

In reflecting on the Hawaiian words Ho' Ano, which means to plant a seed, I realized that to intentionally hurt another person was the worst thing to do. These words always take me back to their meaning. It is a heavy burden to carry anger in your heart as a result of hurt, as it can foster the death of the soul. Bitterness is one of the hardest stages of anger to overcome. The chaos of life can be total destruction. I was on the edge of this emotional presence until I woke up!

"Thomas! I need you!" "Thomas! I need you!"

When it shows its face, all values are compromised: I was imploding and exploding in the moment. All my gifts were shut down. In these moments, I had no compassion, joy, or empathy. I was angry, hurt, and confounded.

The polarity of the extremes was sitting on the fence... I needed to make a choice!

An old Indian saying is, "What wolf will I feed? The compassionate wolf or the selfish wolf?"

The battle was intense as I wanted to feed the compassionate wolf. My prophecy was at the crossroads of survival or physical death... literally. The war of two worlds was on a collision course with no turning back if I had not chosen the good wolf.

The cognitive dissonance of two conflicting ideas was at my doorstep as a result of the chaos of inner conflict between two choices.

Quote page 38 jts

"Consciousness through subconscious revelations humbles.

Then may one begin to realize the force from within: love!"

The light had and is still speaking the words: to trust my higher self. I am not alone and surrender my will. The enlightenment has grounded me... the rock, Mother Earth, my anchor.

Aramaic Lord's prayer quote

"O Cosmic Birther of all radiance (light) and vibration (love is the energy field).

Soften the ground of our being (body) and carve out a space within us (the heart)

where your presence (life force/creator) can abide.

For you are the ground, and the fruitful vision, the birth, power, and fulfillment, as

all is gathered and made whole again."

And so, it is!!!

All (God) is the light, and love is the energy field of change. When embraced, one's purpose is consciously pursued. Joy and

peace are the way of life that keeps one on their path... karma.

Quote

p18 jts

"Just to sit

allows silence to calm one

so peace can enter

to soothe the soul."

****

Even out of darkness comes light. No one tribe owns everything. Consciousness is symbolized by the light of the day... the sun. Even in the extreme darkness, there is the light of the stars and the moon... releasing insights on the path of enlightenment when seeking understanding. Salvation is a promise. It is the clearing in the forest (meaning a meadow, and that is what my last name means). The ways and means of fulfilling our destiny are at their best when in the moment.

The joy and peace felt is the discovery of our longing to know the truth. The clearing feeds the mind, body, and soul for the good of all. An awareness that is rooted in our heart and in the silence of actions always speaks louder than words.

Quote page 20 jts

"The Heart always speaks under the Word"

****

The center of enlightenment is facilitated by the heart. Removing the darkness of our essence by the conscious awareness of an awe-inspired reverence that unties the tangled threads of destiny that bind us, as we release others from past mistakes... achieved by forgiveness of others and including ourselves. This truth is the humble moment of awareness.

As I ask my creator... show me... show me... show me. Do not let me be seduced by that which would divert me from my true purpose. Wrapping all that cross my path in love and light, placing them in the creator's hands for illumination of the present moment. Liberating one from the chains of bondage of our past... allowing one to move forward.

Thom's

"Truth has no shadows."

Quote page 19 jts

"You cannot keep hurting

a person you love,

and expect them to keep

liking you."

Thom's

"Peace is the union of

the male and female essence

of oneness—balance."

Quote page 43 jts

"As long as the mind believes

what it was taught to be good

without questioning,

it could be a deficit

to our joy and peace,

as it may not be true."

****

The revelation was liberating. I started to understand my ego. As my ego had become a defense mechanism, embraced and used when caught in situations of defense for mannerisms learned without a clue to understand or discern current moments of chaos caused by ignorance, anger, guilt, etc.!

These taught patterns came from the subconscious when provoked. The fear is demoralizing. Protecting my feelings was paramount. I had serious deficits. I was humbled after all the shocks from the prophecy. Now I look at them through a different lens.

I was haunted by my reactions to threatening events, often when I was living alone and reflecting on life... known as a bad hair day. I would look into my mirror and say, "How are you going to rationalize these thoughts?" These observations were very eye-opening. I could project none of my reactions on anyone. What a major shift in thinking started to emerge! A deep sense of awareness came over me and still does as I am clearing my path and walking to the light... true discernment was the point. The other side of midnight had started to come into play.

Quote page 38 jts

"Consciousness through

subconscious revelation humbles.

Then may one begin to realize

the force from within.

Love."

Immediately recalling my partner's reaction was the waving of his arm back and forth as he snapped his fingers... saying, "Get over yourself. If you carry on like this after I pass, I shall haunt your ass!" I smile and laugh when in this space. It is so humbling and grounding.

I am just another soul trying to understand and be a good person. The person I have to forgive the most is myself! As I really did do it! I came to the planet of slow learners, and I am that person at times. Please! "Stop in the name of love."

****

Now I have more means to address my shadows when ego tries to take over. Less time in the malaise of chaos allows me to return quicker to my happy space as I strive to stay on the road less traveled. I am not anyone's savior.

Reality for me is the moment of awareness that changes me for the greater good of all. Remember, I am still in preschool.

Quote page 29 jts

A New Dawn

"Obedience to truth

neutralizes corruption."

Quote page 20 jts

"Do not be upset,

things do get better.

It may be stormy now,

but it cannot rain forever."

****

Take a break... it's time to pause. Joy is filling my being. Carry on! Move forward; the past is coming closer. As the entanglement of the threads of destiny that connect us is being untied, releasing one from past mistakes. The forgiving presence silently engages, allowing us to shed the veil of our dark shadows. The energy fields of radiance (light) and vibration (love) are means to balance one.

Comic relief was one means of shifting, as I had just been to Hero's Comicon in Charlotte, North Carolina. A sense of peace and release had manifested; I left the land of chaos in this moment and visited Fantasy Island. What an awesome intermission.

****

After the Comicon, a series of events started to surface from my subconscious in the dream state.

My dreams up to this time were very nonsensical and lost as I was awakening. No more; my dreams became vivid and meaningful in recall. As they grounded me, revealing in detail a meaning in reference to my prophecy.

The first Dream started with Silver Coins of all enominations.

In the dream, I was scrambling all over a brick courtyard, collecting silver coins from nickels, dimes, quarters, fifty-cent pieces, and silver dollars. Hurriedly grabbing the coins as if it were my last chance, I lacked understanding of why I was collecting them so fanatically.

Instantly, I looked up and saw a lady in profile with a scarf over her hair. Her hand was extended, wanting me to give her the coins. Glancing at her, I backed away, clutching the coins and feeling I should share. My reaction was automatic, and I pulled back my hand. I emphatically said "NO," shaking my head as I turned my back on her and continued gathering more silver coins.

The first impression I received was one of deception. She spoke no words; the coins were for me. I finally gave myself permission to use what was given to me, and I felt no guilt.

Silver was an intuitive symbol of betrayal. My great-great-grandmother of my prophecy was that lady with the extended hand. Recalling her words, "Tomas is a small gift, being a caretaker," I realized I was not following my destiny. I was out to save the world one person at a time. OMG! I am not the savior.

I was sensitive and wanting to alleviate their pain and troubles.

The first Dream started with Silver Coins of all enominations.
In reality, the energy was a reflection of ties that opened the door to energy fields of greed and taking advantage of my empathic and giving nature. I was spinning in the wheels of life, going nowhere. I finally understood my deficit: my ego!

Turning away was the first step needed to start a new approach to comprehend the courtyard experience. New avenues were opening through this dream. I realized I was lost.

Lord's Prayer in Aramaic

"Do not let us be seduced by that which diverts us from our true purpose, but illuminate for us the opportunities of the present moment."

Quote page 26 jts

"In the moment, all answers are possible."

****

The Prophecy is now the center of my awareness. She (grandmother) was calling me. The confusion and the chaos of my mind was like a wobbling of the wheels of life on a crash course. Lost for words, I started to ingest her words seriously. "You receive, but you don't put action in place. He (Tomas) is Tchatche (small gift) that is meant to be more but receives but does not follow the path of Enlightenment. Chooses to be small by being a caregiver, allowing to be used to make himself all important."

I finally digested her Prophecy. Hence, I turned my back on the lady. The dream's revelation was point on. I was not living my Karma. The need to return to my purpose is a must for personal fulfillment. I am only a messenger sharing and charging the Earth's Grid with Intuits received from the Universe.

This was an AHA moment!

Quote from the prophecy:

The first Dream started with Silver Coins of all enominations.
"If I (grandmother) had wheels, I would be a wagon…"

Meaning, don't expect people to do things they aren't equipped to do. Dogs can be trained to love and follow. Man uses those who do not see but their own importance, which is melting Ice (fading away, passing as a changing form) as in a slow death and not completing one's Karma.

Her message was very upsetting at first. I was in shock, believing I was helping people. Instead, I went too far. In reality, I (assumed) they understood me. Instead, many thought I was out on a limb, far removed from their reality.

Finally, I started to break down my observations and discerned the meaning that she shared to awaken me. You are a messenger only; back off when the message is delivered.

The Ego was a real obstacle for me. I shared with good intentions. I was looked at as different.

Immediately, the word humble had a whole new meaning. I stood back and observed the consequences of assumptions. As awareness grew, it still took over 2½ years to understand most of the basic message.

And the unraveling of the prophecy is still a work in progress.

****

The weight of the journey is falling off as consciousness is my focal point as I remove the veil over my eyes and heart. An awe-inspired reverence was growing in me as I was humbled, and conscious awareness was now a mainstay of the present moment. I am not threatened by fear, guilt, and shame as I once was. Love and light are my grounding energy fields that emanate from my heart and aura.

Being humble was the words of freedom as I surrender my will to my higher self, asking my creator to make me worthy of my purpose so that I can fulfill my karma as a child of light and love as a messenger. Even if I never speak a word again, my actions can speak louder than words.

Show me... Show me... Show me... as I face the shadows of life that emerge from thee echoes of my mind. Thank you, Lord, for the light on the road less traveled that opened my heart to the truth.

****

Great Grandmother visited again! Appearing in a beautiful green, red, and purple silk turban.

From her profile, I saw a 24-karat gold earring. A regal woman who bore my father's father, who was of gentle strength and caring. He was diverted from his way, and like melting ice, he was fading. My great-grandfather took his own life. He had lost his light, and I don't know if I shall ever understand all that happened to him to reach this decision. Passing on the attributes of the family before him were weakened to a point of no return. His shadows had consumed him.

As I stood at his grave in 2005 on my return to Michigan, I am now reflecting on my feelings of the revelations. I feel the light and the love that was given to my ancestors and to me as I faced my shadows that could end my purpose too. I do not have to dig any deeper into the family secrets. I have seen and felt enough. The diversion from my true path was over in my heart. Now I am building that bridge to return to my path as I am conscious of the fall of my family. Let me use the gifts we, as a family, were given to live a better life and to release the messages that are channeled through me into the world as I was meant to do.

My father was a wonderful soul. He had this twinkle in his piercing sky-blue eyes when his heart was on course. His light and love just emanated from him, and magic flowed as he was in a state of bliss.

The intuitions my father shared were simplistic and profound, more so now. As the words are riveting as they ricochet from facet to facet and are forever etched in my heart from the echoes of my mind. He laid the groundwork for my walk with the intention to make a better life for his children, as my mother did in her own way. Their strength is in me, and when used for the good of all, it is beyond words. The heart is the vehicle of bridging the higher self and his children. My parents together gave us the means to achieve our purpose.

****

After I returned to Michigan, my mother and I discussed and shared insights on their relationship and their upbringing. I knew their love was mutual for us siblings. They promoted the gift of possibilities through their thoughts, words, and actions. By living their kindness, a genuine hope for us also included other people besides family.

This foundation brought forth my seeking of the meaning of life and my belief in my higher self. As the Creator showed me the way to live a good life, no matter what I have to experience to understand and own my life lessons, I have arrived! Enlightenment is my choice. I jumped on the wagon, and I am moving and have returned to the road less traveled— my karma and reason for living on the good earth. Go within and listen to the spirit of all—the Alpha and the Omega. Life is not always easy! But when embraced, it humbles one with an awareness and shines without speaking a word.

****

Joy and Peace

Quote page 6 jts

"All we need is right in front of us.

In the complexities of seeking,

the simplistic opens the window

of opportunity to understand

that which gives us peace.

Allowing the ultimate energy of consciousness

to show us that random acts of kindness

are the keys that propel us forward

in understanding of life situations.

Witnessing change brings awareness,

then the insights of bigger shifts.

The result can be phenomenal when engaged."

****

After my dream, I started to recall more as I was beginning to see a pattern to the revelations. The reflections of other dreams are now in my consciousness, reaffirming me again. My prophecy is a wake-up call. I was lost in the chaos of the world,

The first Dream started with Silver Coins of all enominations.
and now I see how it diverted me from personal advancements on my journey. It is the time of awakening to follow my true path and do the will of my Creator, who asks me to charge the grids of the Earth so mankind can be released from the limitations of man's deception to control others and share the intuitions that are channeled through me. I am just the messenger!

The Thunderbird Vision

On the wings of the Thunderbird happened long before the prophecy. The intuit I received was a result of being drawn to a shaman that I met in a health food store. Never expecting I would be curious enough to engage in their ways of connecting with the Great Spirit.

Needless to say, the session was the precursor of what was to materialize. During the session, as I engaged with him, I was in flight, sitting on what I called an eagle out of the corner of my eye in a free-fall dive. All of a sudden, I realized it was not an eagle. This could not be, as a human, I was too big and heavy. Instantly, I realized it was the mystical Thunderbird of Native American culture.

In their beliefs, it is a powerful mystical creature representing strength, protection, and a force of nature. Generally considered the connection between heaven and Earth, it intervenes on behalf of humans.

At the end of the session with the shaman, he was awestruck, as he had never experienced the Thunderbird. He gave me a message with such passion. Emphatically, he said, "Please do not leave this Earth." He said it several times. His response was imprinted on my mind and stored in my subconscious. Often, I would reflect on the session until it faded. I forgot about this vision.

Quote page 14 jts

"Vibrational consciousness is different.

Like vibration connections create.

Anything is possible.

Different vibrations in one's path

intuitively sensed.

Interpretation as a course of action

at the moment needs not always

be understood.

Just file in your memories until needed."

****

One day, as I was entering a food market, I decided to buy a pastry as a treat. Approaching the bakery, I was devouring the display, trying to decide which pastry I was craving. All of a sudden, I felt a powerful attraction and noticed a person near me. It was like a bolt of lightning struck me. I felt the electrifying energy between us. It was one of unbelievable pain and a state of loss. When the person looked up at me, I felt a profound need to hug them. Immediately, the feeling was mutual, as it was spoken in unspoken words.

A conversation was engaged, and I knew I wanted to talk more. Being in a hurry, I had to return to work, so I exchanged my phone number. As I turned to leave, the Thunderbird passed over us, turning and saying, "I shall call soon."

As I am sharing, I recall the symbolism of the Thunderbird. To repeat, it is generally considered a guardian spirit with the ability to intervene on behalf of a human.

Immediately, I understood the vision as the precursor of my prophecy. Recalling the caregiver in me now gripped me and locked me in the moment of total awareness, understanding, and owning the meaning: you are a small gift (Tahache), calling forth the consequence of staying in that mindset. I feel like melting ice... I am fading. Hence the shaman's message: "Please do not leave the Earth. The Earth needs you!"

The Holy Spirit spoke to me: "Thomas! I need you! Thomas! I need you!"

I am running with this insight. I chose the will of my Creator. Show me… show me… show me!

The HO' ANO… the seeds were planted in Hawaii and were being nourished. As I experienced the necessary moment to bring the seed to fruition, I accepted my truth, and now I am running with it. The seeds are the means to share as I receive and debunk the shadows that keep me in bondage to the limitations of man's controls and others too! The heavy shadows of ignorance produced by man and my self-protector, my ego… I finally know more means to put it in check faster.

Quote page 36 jts

"Until we balance our soul,

events do not change.

Demonstrations are changing;

situations become more intense,

demanding, and felt.

Until the soul integrates truth."

Quote page 40 jts

"One cannot extract from another

anything that one has not

removed from themselves."

Quote page 41jts

"When facing life,

ask what it is teaching you,

not what it is taking from you."

****

An awe-inspired reverence has now been stamped on my heart. The hallowedness of my awakening—light and love— has made these words among the most important keys of my journey. Along with humbleness, these two words coalesce as the grounding anchors of consciousness, understanding, and ownership of one's purpose. Light and love are the energy fields that facilitate bringing the stored shadows of darkness in the subconscious, which hold one back from the truth that can free us. "As above, so below," love and light conquer all. Ask what one will of all, and all will… show me… show me… show me.

"The heart is calling."

"The heart always speaks under the words."

I can never share this enough!

****

I had to choose my karma or remain in the darkness of my shadows. Oh! Hell... I wanted my PhD and to get the hell out of Dodge when ready to return home to my Creator.

Aramaic Lord's Prayer

"Do not let me be seduced

by that which diverts us from our true purpose,

but illuminate the opportunities of the present moment."

****

As the Native Americans would say… what wolf would you feed? The wolf of love and light, truth? Or the wolf of deception, dark shadows, or lies?

All recalled from the echoes of my mind. Hence, the emancipation of the mind. The subconscious is the storage cloud of all that I am, containing the good, the bad, and the indifferent—the aspects of oneself when realized.

Quote page 8 jts

"Ego is the defense mechanism

employed when lacking insights

to understand truth."

Quote page 9 jts

"Play safe

like a reprieve,

a chance to relax

to catch the breath.

Energy moves forward.

A glimpse allows the move,

by just being aware."

****

The Coyote Dream

Dreaming was not insightful until now. All my dreams started to be vivid, and remembering was the difference. Then the questioning and reflecting increased in the search for meaning.

The coyote dream was gnawing at me, as I had never looked at them as insightful. Until I woke up one morning being attacked by a pack of coyotes biting at my heels. The bites were painful.

From this moment on, I started to seek understanding as to what they were revealing to me. In my research, I found the use of the word "Trickster." Deception was the word of reference—they were warning me. The biting scared me more than the hurting. My prophecy was in my face: "You are fading... like melting ice." I did not understand the words. The reoccurrence of the phrase started to reveal itself. I am lost in the chaos of deceit. Man's ways were seducing me and diverting me from my path. Thee echoes of my mind were aggressively gnawing at me... like the biting of heels.

"Wake up! Wake up!" is the essence of the biting. Return to your purpose. Stop being a caretaker at the expense of your purpose. My ego was being challenged by my ignorance of not knowing how this started. You are here to charge the grids of the Earth by sharing the intuitions that are given to you and then move on. You, Thomas, need to honor your purpose.

Thomas, you are sharing the means to ponder so others can develop the wisdom of their soul and share what each being needs to grow and flourish. A shared consciousness is understood when they are receptive, resulting in each soul walking their own path as they understand it and own it. This awareness contributes to uniting the oneness of the collective consciousness of the Higher Self—the cosmic birther, the essence of all that is gathered and made whole again.

As we piece our lessons together, the truth has no shadows. It never changes, and one can continue on their path with joy and peace. The means to progress are expanding through the light of awakening and the energy fields of love that connect all of us. This is not fantasy for me. My dreams and intuitions anchored and returned me to my path, even with the walls of shadows blocking me. I return to the light and love, as they freed me to return to my path of liberation.

Quote page 17jts

"The beauty of failure is

rebirth, a clean slate."

Quote page 35 jts

"Peace is a continuous act

of loving the world."

Quote

"I know I am,

as I know we are.

One in purpose.

Love."

Yes, the coyotes are omens of dark shadows that cross our path—to be faced through self-reflection as a means of transformation to return to our journey of purpose. I am feeling good! I can see clearer now! I am moving forward, and I am not going back—embracing the challenge as well as the good times.

I am no longer a sparrow (a small gift). I choose to be an eagle, soaring in the sky between the universe and the Earth, collecting the information needed to be enlightened on the good Earth.

✳✳

Intermission—a shift in consciousness and grounding. The most symbolic moment was the morning I woke up. I was outside on my lanai when a pair of red cardinals flew by in my presence. The angels had returned... my messengers. As I didn't heed my intuitions, they could not come anymore; they could only watch. Having accepted my destiny, I released my will to my higher self and pursued enlightenment versus the shadows that my ego was guarding due to my ignorance and the stroking of my ego that fed the limits of darkness.

Truly, I thought I was helping people, not realizing others have the right to choose their own path... free will... step aside.

✳✳

The Golden Cobra Dream

Again, I woke up from a dream screaming, "What is this all about?" A brilliant 24-karat gold cobra was fiercely attacking me, barely missing. Finally, I recognized my delusional ill as a result of the chaos of my ego—a defense mechanism from my childhood to the present moment, all stored in my subconscious. The reflection had become a constant reminder of my inability to grasp the know-how of exposing my ego to light and understanding that would allow me an opportunity for deliverance through enlightenment.

Contemplating my prophecy led me to the keys for releasing myself to my true path. Aided by the movies of my life and the dreams that brought forth intuitions of change, I moved from recorded memories to a conscious state of awareness that emanated from fear. A prisoner of the mind, the emotions were strangling deficits that could destroy the soul.

All that glitters is not gold. Success is not just how much bling one can hold in their hands. It is the content of the heart from which the light and love radiate and vibrate that is honored. This is the gold standard of life and the most precious state of being when owned. It is the golden aura of true essence.

The golden cobra pulled back, ceasing to strike. The angels were sparkles of light surrounding me. I knew I was on my true path... consciously, and I am humbled.

It has been a long, arduous journey of the heart. The shadows of darkness are fading to the light of love. The bonds of oneness are real. I strive to keep my eyes and heart open. I am alive! My perceptions are keener and at my fingertips, ready to respond quickly—more often than not—to the shadows that challenge us. I am ready to forgive others and especially myself, as everyone needs to be heard.

Quote page 43 jts

"As long as the mind believes what it is taught

to be good without understanding,

it can be a deficit to our joy and peace,

as it may not be true."

****

Scott Peck wrote on this concept in his book, People of the Lie: a phenomenal expression of the idea that negative attention is better than none.

Chaos reigns until the emancipation of the mind is achieved. It is a gateway to conscious living. Stop the insanity; there is no need to beat oneself up.

Reflecting many times and in many different ways to achieve this truth, grounding was facilitated most effectively by going within to the eye of the nous (the heart). It became my go-to place where the soul is nourished, as well as the mind and body.

No longer am I wandering aimlessly. My purpose is clear: stand up for truth. I would lose my life, then my soul (oh! I'm not ready to die).

Truth is the source—from one's higher self, the leader of the pack!

As one enters the real fields of gold, singing the sounds of enlightenment, they move on...

The Messenger.

****

One day, I was sitting on my lanai, and as I looked up, a small golden bee was staring into my eyes. It had never happened before. As I researched it, I found out that my forefathers were beekeepers—symbolic of their drive as a family to produce honey, often called liquid gold. Bees work together to build their home, and their loyalty to the queen is until death, passing on their traits and their oneness of consciousness.

The honey also represents the most important meaning of their gentle strength and caring. My father's father was wombed by my five times removed great-grandmother, and the gift came from them. Grandmother was mémère—not old granny—the queen bee!

My destiny is to remove the prophecy of the melting ice and fading, as in dying. I am no longer a small gift; I am an eagle that receives the messages to be shared with the universe and the good earth from our Creator—the wisdom and spirit that guides me.

Knowing now, I am working tirelessly to earn my PhD of life so I can earn my wings and return home to my Creator.

The joy and peace I hold in my heart is the best gift ever.

"The heart of love hugs me,

as the winds of change

lift me up...

howling.

Sing the song of love,

hugs me again...

releases me... whispering!

Carry on;

love conquers all."

****

Out of many comes one... all.

The Alpha and the Omega.

We are no longer just a village of likeness. We have become a city of lights, unified for the good of All (Alpha and Omega: The Beginning and the End).

We all get lost. Now we are building a way as the opportunities for illumination are upon us. Carry on, as it is heartfelt.

—Thom

www.ingramcontent.com/pod-product-compliance
Lightning Source LLC
Chambersburg PA
CBHW020335130626
46549CB00003B/1185